The Beautiful and Enduring Ozarks

Leland Payton

THE BEAUTIFUL AND ENDURING OZARKS

➜ Lens & Pen Press ◄

For Rollie and Bettina Sparrowe
True friends of the Ozarks and its people

Published by Lens & Pen Press
3020 S. National, #340
Springfield, MO 65804

Email payton@beautifulozarks.com
Web site www.beautifulozarks.com

Library of Congress Catalog Card Number: 99-65982
Electronic typesetting by Ross Daniels Payton
Edited by Crystal Payton
Printed in Singapore
First Edition
ISBN 0-9673925-0-0

Ozark gigger, Vance Randolph photograph, 1930s
(Lyons Memorial Library, College of the Ozarks)

CONTENTS

1. Placing the Ozarks

Few places in the United States have such a vivid popular image as the Ozarks. Farmlands grow our food, factories make our merchandise, and suburbia warehouses our after-work bodies. There is little to distinguish one functional and expedient development from another. Much of the newer America lacks character. There is as yet little mythos or art about it. The old great cities combine geography and history in a signal way. Spaces and natural places heroically defiant of human purpose - canyons, mountain ranges, rocky seacoasts - are sights celebrated in paintings and pictured on postcards. Yet this modest, river-cut, uplifted plateau in the central United States has long had a distinct image, though thinly populated and of small economic import.

There is a variety of sources of Ozark imagery. Poets, free-lance writers, journalists, conservationists, promoters of tourism, sellers of real estate, utopians, scientists, and government bureaucrats have generated photographs, prose, reports, rhetoric, and rhyme about the place for nearly two centuries. All have used pretty much the same raw materials. In choosing the components, the various laborers at this enterprise have been selective. They've picked the more irregular pieces of both the landscape and the populace. Hills and hillfolk are more colorful than the relatively flat parts and the hard working citizens who inhabit the plateau farms and small towns.

Since the area's incorporation into the United States in the early 1800s, the mythic potential and dazzling beauty of the steeper hills along the rivers have been celebrated. The half-wild hunters who stalked these forested breaks were recognized early on as the raw material of legend. It helped immensely that the buckskin-clad frontiersmen were themselves superb storytellers and balladeers of rare voice. The deep Ozarks was associated with these free spirits from the get-go. The social usefulness of these pioneer types dwindled in time and they became stereotyped as hillbillies. But even that socially incorrect pop culture cartoon has some qualities that are not necessarily negative. If nothing else, the hillbilly is funny and musical. If naïve and close-minded about progress, the mythical Ozarker is open to the discrete, anti-

▶ **A Niangua River farm with classic Ozarkian combination of forested hills, bottomland fields, and cliffs with a pure wilderness flora and fauna.**

With the increasing distance interposed by time and space there yet remain forever green the scenes of early years. The old white church, astride its rocky point, overtopped by cedars that grow on the warm rock ledges, forever looks forth upon the fairest valley. The lower slopes are abloom with red clover, or golden with wheat. Wide fields of blue-green corn border the shaded stream, where the bass lurk in transparent pools. In the distance forests of oak mantle the hillsides, up which, past spacious farmhouses, the country roads wind. The people who move upon the scene of this account are homefolks one and all.

Geography of the Ozark Highland of Missouri,
Carl O. Sauer, 1920

bourgeois pleasures of leisure, liquor, and love.

The Ozarks is one of those famous regions whose image is a mixture of culture and geography. Placing the Ozarks on a map is easy. It's an irregular lump in the center of the United States. Most of its 60,000 square miles is in southern Missouri and northern Arkansas. A sizeable hunk of northeastern Oklahoma and a tad of Kansas are parts of the Ozarkian uplift. If it were a state, it would be bigger than Illinois or Florida. It's bounded by the Missouri River on the north, the Mississippi on the east, the Arkansas River on the south. Its western margin is the least distinct as the uplift merges into the plains that run tabletop flat to the Rocky Mountains. But if you're traveling west, leaving the rolling prairie country of Illinois, don't expect a rock shock. Highway engineers hate drama.

Venture off the Interstate or an improved modern highway and the place changes. Gently rolling hills begin to deepen. Pasture becomes forest. Cows and chickens are replaced by deer and wild turkey. After miles of oak-hickory forest, the road, which has assiduously avoided the river, must finally confront it. The cedar-studded canyons, through which the free-flowing waters run, are a shock to citified senses.

That such beauty exists and has endured the crawling chaotic sprawl of our times astonishes me. Ozark streams, and the rough country along them, are places I've been drawn to all my life. When I was young I took a sketchpad, later a camera. Back home, I hunted up books

and magazine articles about the region. Now I have a book about the interaction of literature and geography in my life and about people I've met and about some scaly critters that live under rocks and riffles of the Ozarks. Someone, years from now, will publish another book. I'm not the first to be struck by its wild beauty or taken by the durable character of its inhabitants. I won't be the last to wonder about this place. For the deep Ozarks is a place worth visiting, worth writing about, and worth picturing - and impossible not to think about in between.

▼ A few remnants of native prairie grasses, like big and little bluestem and prairie dropseed, can be found in country churchyards and cemetery grounds.

◄ The plateau parts of the Ozarks were once prairie. Lightning and Indians ignited them, which kept the forests that covered the hills from invading. They were plowed in the 19th century to grow crops. Today, the flatter Ozarks is mostly pasture. This is Friendly Prairie, a relic on the northwest Ozark border preserved by the Missouri Prairie Foundation.

Streams naturally develop a very sinuous path on flat lands. Geologists believe the looping curves of Ozark rivers were formed in a similar fashion to this prairie branch when the entire Ozarks was a low level plain. When the peneplain was slowly uplifted 65 million years ago, the curving forms of the existing rivers were engraved into the limestone bedrock. These river forms, inherited from an earlier geomorphic cycle, are known as entrenched meanders.

◀ Taberville Prairie, at the western edge of the Ozarks, after a prescribed burn. Although the Missouri Department of Conservation has waged a long war against the native tradition of firing the Ozarks to encourage grass, the Department regularly ignites the prairie to discourage woody invasion.

▼ Native grass along the Osage before Truman Dam impounded the river.

The Ozarks is the westernmost extension of the eastern deciduous forest. The pattern of grasslands on the leveler parts and woods occupying the hill sections is essentially unchanged since Indian times. Tame pasture has replaced native prairie and the trees are second or third growth. The gigantic virgin oaks and huge stands of pure pine were a valuable resource largely cut by the turn of the century. Only in certain preserved public lands can we still get a sense of the beauty of the old Ozark forest.

▲ Fire towers no longer dot the skyline but the controversy over the appropriate use and destructive abuse of set fires remains an unresolved issue.

◀ This limestone bluff in Mingo National Wildlife Refuge marks the boundary of the Ozark highlands with the Mississippi lowlands. The richest forest flora is in the southeast margin of the Ozarks. To the oak and hickory mix are added some southern species such as cypress, gum, pecan, and an occasional eastern beech.

Springfield, the largest semi-city in the region, is inordinately attached to the word "Ozarks." Yet, for the most part, it has little to do with the various anachronisms of the back country. Springfieldians are progressive, mercantilist, acquisitive. Their passion for business-like uniformity has resulted in a town that could be anywhere in the vast level Mississippi valley. Winning at sports, even winning at fishing, is big. There is a Sports Hall of Fame here, a sports newspaper, and the city is the headquarters of Bass Pro, a nationwide chain of stores themed on the competitive game of catching, weighing, and releasing largemouth bass in Corps of Engineers reservoirs. Money is how score is kept in Springfield, as it is in most such developer-banker-and-bureaucrat run towns.

Branson, the tourist mecca 40 miles south, has a toe-tapping, thigh-slapping, good old country music foundation (recently leavened by pop culture acts) but it's often snubbed by Springfield's progressive and "arty" gentry. In general, Springfield, like most up-to-date communities, does not honor individuality and differentness—except, of course, for the *au courant*, middle class fixation on "multicultural diversity." Yet the media swoons at the sound of the word and the Springfield Yellow Pages are full of "Ozarks" this or that business.

This conflicts, of course, with the mythic Ozarks, a place of wooded hills, inhabited by bedrock conservatives. Disharmony between culture derived from the frontier and progress isn't unique to Springfield. Commercially-minded Americans are quick to paper over the old faded patterns of tradition or to raze a historic structure instead of shoring it up. Both the geography and culture of the old Ozarks have proven to be difficult to modify and naturally resistant to trendy refurbishing. At the core of Ozark imagery is endurance—aesthetic, spiritual, and geologic. Time hasn't stopped flowing in the wild river valleys, but it does seem to have slowed and pooled. The *Springfield News-Leader* bubbles with booster enthusiasm for rapid development, yet curiously its banner proclaims "Tis a pleasure to live in the Ozarks."

Interstate 44 (the old Mother Road, U.S. 66) cuts across the Ozark plateau in a northeast to southwest slash connecting the East to the West. Travelers coping with 18-wheelers, corporate food and lodging, and other roadside improvements indistinguishable from the rest of contemporary America must wonder "Where is the Ozarks portrayed in this book?" Only a few glimpses of the deep valley of the Gasconade indicate the region is distinguishable from the plains of Illinois to the east, or the flat lands of Oklahoma to the west. The undissected limestone tabletop, that the main roads stick to and most of the people live on, is not aesthetically striking nor is it the habitat of the legendary hillman.

There are few, if any, stills in the Ozarks today. A great many whiskey barrels are made in Lebanon, Missouri, from white oaks. The hillfolks who hack the stave bolts (or, more accurately, cut them with chainsaws) don't wear buckskin or homespun anymore. They can get the latest,

▸ **Scattered through the Ozarks are architectural relics of its complete American history. This closed-up store in northern Arkansas was run by the descendants of Silas Turnbo, who wrote poignantly of the pre-Civil War Ozarks. Similar cycles of history occurred through much of the U.S. Rapid change has obliterated evidence of that era elsewhere. Auto safaris on Ozark back roads are trips through time.**

made-in-Macao fashions at Wal Mart. Many have come to live in towns like Lebanon. They rent a double wide or a duplex and work in the small factories and stores in towns along I-44. Their radios are tuned to country. They cannot be counted on to work the first couple of days of deer season. On Memorial Day, they take plastic flowers to little cemeteries on winding gravel roads that cross creeks of dreamlike clarity and heart-stopping beauty.

▶ Springfield, MO, aspiring metropolis of the Ozarks.

Millions of tourists know the Ozarks as a land of lakes. Actually, they are manmade reservoirs of recent origin. Electric companies, early on, took note of the fast fall of the streams. They coveted all that energy, lost in the gurgling rapids and boiling chutes. A small privately-financed dam was built on the White River for hydro-power in 1913, creating Lake Taneycomo. A larger dam on the Osage River created Lake of the Ozarks in 1931. The opposition of the locals who were displaced was of little concern to the power companies or urban interests. The fate of the Ozarkers whose lands were taken and livelihoods were destroyed mattered even less to the federal dam builders a generation later. Armed with the expanded federal power of the New Deal, the best land and some of the oldest Ozark settlements were appropriated by eminent domain.

In some cases a tourist business did eventually develop, but the locals were often not the beneficiaries. The descendants of the settlers had the founding fathers' suspicions of strong central government. These Army

Corps of Engineers dams symbolize outside domination of this once neglected and nearly autonomous region.

Urban tourists were attracted to these great ponds. They gawked at the idle, shabby men whose best farmland now lay under 150 feet of water. The hillfolk gathered at country stores to curse the feds and swap river stories. The fatalistic character and ironic humor of the frontier survived this displacement. After all, their great-grandfathers back in Tennesse and Kentucky had taken the land away from the Indians. Long before that their ancestors had displaced some Northern Irish at the invitation of the English. Then the English stiffened taxes and tariffs and the Scotch-Irish came to America. They grimaced at comic postcards of themselves. They told sarcastic jokes, spit tobacco, and commented on the comeliness of certain of the tourist women. The descendants of frontiersmen had become hillbillies.

▶ Even critics of the Corps of Engineers must concede that Ozark reservoirs like Greers Ferry in Arkansas have high quality water and good fishing and boating.

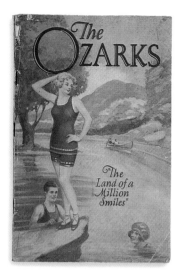

G od used a caressing hand in the Ozarks, creating a vast table land, broken into hundreds of mountain ridges covered with forest and cut by hundreds of whispering brooks and rushing streams which sing their way on to the larger streams beyond. These unselfish little streams, which nose their way into every little district, lest some be slighted, carry their song into every mountain nook and with their magnetic force draw the tourist to their cool banks to fish or swim or listen to the story of the woods and flowers.

The Ozarks: The Land of a Million Smiles,
Ozark Playgrounds Association, 1930

Long before the high dams and impounds of the post World War II era encouraged mass tourism, a few adventurous urban sportsmen had discovered the wild Ozarks. Railroads penetrated the region after the Civil War, allowing access to wilderness hunting and fishing. Improved roads and the automobile brought sightseers and vacationers into the Ozarks in some numbers in the 1920s and 1930s. Scattered through the region today are attractions and parks that preserve the flavor of an Ozark vacation between the two world wars.

Like as not, the kids in the back seat then were Boy Scouts or Camp Fire Girls, indoctrinated with the woods lore and rustic esthetic of the earlier Arts and Crafts movement. The public loved to rough it then. Movies, books, and murals celebrated our pioneer heritage. Family excursions had a decidedly do-it-yourself, discover-early-America flavor. There were show caves to explore and rivers to canoe. Rustic resorts had tennis and horseback riding. Most of the roadside businesses catering to travelers were built of log or stone. Romantic, purple-tinted prose extolled the salubrious quality of the air and the purity of the water.

Headquartered in Joplin, Missouri, the Ozark Playgrounds Association began in 1919 as a cooperative effort of businesses to promote tourism in the region. For many years, it put out an illustrated booklet of the recreational opportunities in southwest Missouri and northwest Arkansas.

The Big Spring, Largest Single Spring in the World

Sun Bathing
In the Beautiful Ozarks

The OZARKS

"The
Land of a
Million
Smiles"

The Old Mill, Alley Spring State Park

on the Current River in the Beautiful Ozarks

Round Spring, Round Spring State Park

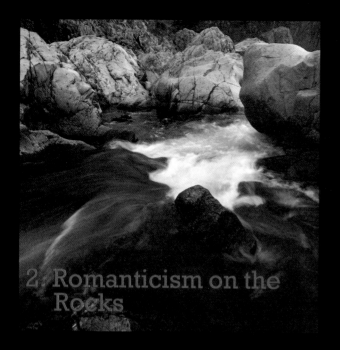

2. Romanticism on the Rocks

Our picture of the Ozarks is framed by romanticism, the dominant art form of the early 19th century when the region was first occupied by Americans. Shelley and Keats didn't write poems on Greer Springs or the bluffs of the Gasconade. Early settlers didn't hold readings of *Ode to a Skylark* by the cabin hearth. But the spirit of early romanticism did color the words of the explorers, travel writers, and even geologists and soldiers who first described the place in English. Such prose clearly reveals the origins of our present attitude toward nature.

This take persists, having found in the wild landscape of the Ozarks perfect subject matter. The flattening, reductional lens of modernism doesn't work here as well as the deep focus, wide-angled glass of romanticism. In time, a popularized aspect of this movement would put on rose-colored filters and render a soft-focus and sentimental portrait of nature and natives. In its prime, however, it was sharp-edged, exploratory, and wide eyed. The high ground of our American vision of nature is a beckoning, but dangerous, horizon, first glimpsed by venturesome romantics.

Untamed nature, primitive people unspoiled by civilization, and revolution were three favored notions of European romanticism. The Louisiana Purchase, that vast wilderness acquired by Thomas Jefferson from France in 1803, had two of the above components. Our wild Eden came with splendid noble savages and a sublime natural backdrop. Americans could easily supply the spirit of revolution themselves. Lewis and Clark's expedition discovered a country worthy of a Byronic epic.

George William Featherstonhaugh, an aristocratic Englishman, traveled through the Ozarks in 1834. In his account, *Excursion Through the Slave States*, he rhapsodically described the rugged scenery and rapped the rugged pioneers for their indifference to his highborn sensitivities. Educated travelers have continued to so appraise the Ozark landscape and its inhabitants.

Hernando De Soto, in 1539, became the first European to seek riches in the rocks of the Ozarks. Finding not gold, but a wealth of hostile natives, the Spanish went elsewhere. Nearly two centuries later, the French exploited the lead and iron resources of the St. Francois Mountains with varying success. Today, the French heritage of the region consists of some place names, a trace of Gaelic folklore, and some diggings, still unsightly after 200 years. The Spanish and French colonial contribution to our perception of the region is negligible.

This was as savage as the wildest nature could make it, and possessed a fearful, yet attractive character. The extent and grandeur of the view, the silence and solitude of the scene, were impressive.

G. W. Featherstonhaugh 1834

Zebulon Pike led a similar, but less well known, exploration to the Southwest wilderness, which began by ascending the Osage River on the northwest flank of the Ozarks. Although a less talented writer than Meriwether Lewis, Pike did enthuse about Indians and the bluffs along the Osage.

Accounts of other educated observers of the region during this era were likewise disposed. In *Excursion Through the Slave States,* an English gentleman/geologist, George Featherstonhaugh, recorded his travels with his son through the eastern margin of the Ozarks in the 1830s. Predictably, he found the log cabin settlers uncouth, and the food not to his liking. Like most literate Europeans and Americans of the period, he extolled the primitive landscape. He reveled in mysterious scenes with a hint of danger: "We were alone, in a country so wild and savage, that if any misfortune happened to us, we would expect no assistance; and the more comfortable consciousness that we were in the possession of health, strength, and resolution, imparted a romantic and exhilarating feeling that made us happy for the moment."

Henry Rowe Schoolcraft's *Journal of a Tour into the Interior of Missouri and Arkansaw . . . 1818-1819* captures the early American take on nature best. Ostensibly a journey to report on the prospects of mining, he indulged his aesthetic passions while neglecting hard economic fact-finding. He would not be the last American to attempt to pass off a book of essentially artistic feeling as a useful guide to development and wealth. True, he did note the diligent mining operation of Moses Austin (who also helped fund his trip) and the careless digging of itinerant frontier types.

Schoolcraft began in Potosi on Thursday, the 5th of November, 1818. By Wednesday, the 11th, he and his traveling companion, Levi Pettibone, had slipped past the lead district and into the Ozark wilderness where they could hear wolves howling 200 yards from their campfire. That day he wrote, "We then entered into lofty forests of pine, and after winding along through valleys and deep defiles of rocks for several miles, found ourselves on the banks of Current's River, in a deep and romantic valley." His journal entry on Thursday, the 12th, begins: "We find ourselves in a highly interesting section of country, and which affords some of the most picturesque and sublime views of rural scenery which I have ever beheld."

The eastern travelers explored Ashley Creek. Schoolcraft likened the limestone bluffs to "towers of some antique ruin." In the many caves he noted the "beauty and regularity" in the arrangement of the colors of stalactites. The place filled him with "awe and astonish-

ment." In two weeks, the young Henry Schoolcraft had grasped the appeal of the wild Ozarks. He rhapsodized about the landscape: "The views which are presented are commanding and delightful, and to the painter who wishes to depict the face of nature in its wildest aspect of rocky grandeur, I could recommend this valley, and the adjacent country, as one of unrivalled attractions."

I recall telling my parents about my Boy Scout campouts and childhood fishing trips with equal, but less articulate, enthusiasm. The voices in my dark woods were barred owls, not timber wolves. All of us who sleep on an Ozark gravel bar by a gurgling, clear river share the dreams that Henry Schoolcraft had in that mild winter of 1818-1819. After a long day's float, chert rocks can be surprisingly comfortable, if it doesn't rain upstream that night.

No birds were present, and it was uninhabited by wild beasts, for the country was of such an arid, siliceous nature, that there was neither water nor herbage, both necessary to the smaller animals, which are the immediate motives that lead the rapacious ones to prowl about.

G. W. Featherstonhaugh, 1834

◀ ▲ Geologists are not immune to the romantic beauty of the riverine Ozark landscape. These lithographs of the Osage River were in an 1873 book published by the Missouri Bureau of Geology and Mines.

The highest elevations in the Ozarks are in the St. Francois Mountains, except for some summits in the Boston Mountains. Ancient fire-formed rocks protrude in patches through the very old sedimentary rocks that form the surface of the rest of the Ozarks. At least a billion years old, these extremely hard granites and rhyolites have created a spectacular landscape, especially where waterways have encountered them. "Streams which flow over the igneous rocks have eroded valleys not much wider than their channels, and their beds are marked by series of rapids. These gorges are impassable, or nearly so, and with their barren walls and turbulent waters afford some of the wildest scenery of the Ozarks." Geographer Carl O. Sauer thus describes "shut-ins".

Commercial minerals are associated with these surface occurrences of Precambrian rocks. The gold- and silver-obsessed Spanish explored the Mississippi valley in the 16th century. After that, French explorers, priests, fur traders, miners, and con artists attempted to exploit and possess the interior of North America. They were notably better in dealing with intractable Indians. Needing the martial skills of the Osage tribe, the French courted them with firearms, iron axes, and even occasional trips to France. The warriors returned with stories of having been "married" to ladies of the court many times.

At one point in this era, Ozark rocks became fragments of one of history's grandest stock swindles. In 1717, John Law, a Scot, gained a commercial monopoly in Louisiana and formed the *Compagnie d'Occident*, also known as the Mississippi Company. He sold shares in the company which would, investors were told, harvest untold wealth from the wilds of America. Although the St. Francois Mountains hold one of the earth's richest deposits of lead (and substantial quantities of zinc, iron, and other minerals), the recovery of its silver awaited 20th century technology. So, the company's agent, Sieur de Lochon, salted silver into the forty pounds of lead he carried from his Meramec River smelter to Paris. The silver excited speculators and they advanced more money. This so-called Mississippi Bubble collapsed in October of 1720, ruining many French aristocratic investors.

The French did later reconcile themselves to the more prosaic, but marginally profitable, lead mining, but legends of lost silver mines are still a fixture of Ozark folklore. Fraudulent misrepresentation of the prospects of easy and vast profit from the rocks of the Ozarks have not vanished, either.

Next two pages: The White River and one of its principal tributaries, the Buffalo River.

I came upon the valley of White River, in Arkansas, which in some places is very broad, and cuts those highlands into two distinct portions. This stream, which is very little known in the Atlantic states, is one of the most important and beautiful rivers in the United States. It takes its rise in the western edge of that elevated country which has received the designation of Ozark Mountains, and receives several important tributaries

G.W. Featherstonhaugh, 1834

T hese people who called themselves the Little Ones, had great height, consummate artistry in bluff and aggressiveness, and could hold their rich domain against all invaders.

The Osages, Children of the Middle Waters, John Joseph Mathews, 1961

Henry Schoolcraft's lifework would be recording Indian culture, but he encountered only some deserted villages in his tour through the Ozarks in 1818-1819. The Osage tribe possessed the region when President Jefferson paid Napoleon 15 million dollars for the vast Louisiana Purchase in 1803. For a few decades, they returned in small bands to hunt, but there were few incidents of violence between Americans and Osages. Having contended with the Spanish, and traded extensively with

the French, the Osages had developed considerable sophistication in dealing with white men.

Delaware, Shawnee, and other eastern tribes, displaced by American settlements, were overrunning Osage territories and depleting the game. A trickle of white hunters preceded a horde of settlers across the Mississippi and into the Ozark river valleys. Sadly, but realistically, the Osages ceded the vast territory between the Missouri and the Arkansas Rivers. In 1808, they peaceably, but reluctantly, moved westward into Kansas Territory.

When land hungry settlers desired the prairies of eastern Kansas, the Osages were moved into arid northeastern Oklahoma. Fortuitously, a vast pool of oil lay under the dry scrub country. Most of the oil has now been removed, but for a time in the 1920s, the Osages became, per capita, one of the richest peoples on earth. Astute tribal elders had refused to give up the mineral rights to the sterile, rocky reservation.

▲ Wa-Sho'-She, late 1800s photograph of an Osage of the Eagle Gens. When George Catlin, the artist, visited the tribe in 1811, he described them as being "so tall and robust as to warrant of the term gigantic: few of them appear under six feet, and many are above it."

◄ For well over ten thousand years, the Ozarks was home to Indians. Little is known of this long history. A few chipped flint tools do not tell a detailed story.

3. Clear and Rushing Waters

The waters of the Ozark highlands are as transparent as the surrounding big rivers are turbid. Deceptively transparent. Schoolcraft discovered this when attempting to ford a clear, shallow stream. Their pack horse plunged in over his head, "by which our baggage got completely wetted. Our tea, meal, salt, sugar etc was either greatly damaged, or entirely spoiled; our skins, blankets, and clothing, were also soaked with water, and such part of our powder as was not bottled shared the same fate."

Every floater today relives these magical illusions. The superior qualities of Ozark water have long been noted. "Good water for whiskey," rejoiced the Scotch-Irish pioneers. "Good smallmouth bass habitat," reported sportsmen who discovered the excellent smallmouth bass fishing in the late 1800s. Where the big springs pour out frigid, clear water, trout could also be transplanted.

Spring water's medicinal qualities didn't stand scientific testing, but for a time, quacks successfully sold the idea that sipping or soaking in their spring water would cure what ailed you. Eureka Springs got its start in the spa era. There were many other promotions of the curative qualities of Ozark waters, most now forgotten.

The energy with which the rivers of the Ozarks flowed was capitalized on early. Running water will turn machinery, if properly harnessed. Peppered across the Ozarks today are the ruins of mills built to grind grain and saw logs. Out of the hundreds that were constructed, a handful still exist. The surviving old mills draw tourists, as they once attracted settlers.

Grander utilization of the Ozark rivers was envisioned. Contrary to popular conception, there were a few ambitious pioneer developers. Among the hunters and small farmers were men who intended to transform the place, to improve it, and to prosper along with the rest of progressive America. Waterways needed to be improved.

Impediments to barge and steamboat travel had to be removed. So essential were channel-

The extreme limpidity of the water of this
stream gives rise to a species of deception of
which we have this day had a serious proof. It is so
clear, white, and transparent, that the stones and
pebbles in its bottom, at a depth of eight of ten
feet, are reflected through it with the most perfect
accuracy as to colour, size, and position, and at the
same time appear as if within two or three feet of
the surface of the water.

   Henry R. Schoolcraft, 1818

deepening and snag-sawing that the expenditure of public money was justified. The Army Corps of Engineers was formed in 1802 to accomplish the improvement of the nation's waterways. By the time the Ozarks was settled, the industry of developing our nation's rivers for the public good, with the largesse of public money, was well established.

Except for the two largest rivers, the Osage and the White, there was little hope that Ozark rivers could be improved. Highland streams are swift and shallow. More importantly, even if they had miraculously become deep and dependable waterways, they didn't connect major commercial centers. Logs were floated efficiently down-stream in high water. Deer hides, wild honey, and bear fat could be canoed from the headwaters and rafted down the lower stretches of the rivers. Small steamboats could ascend the Osage River to Warsaw, and the White River to Forsyth, with minimal deepening and clearing of snags. By the time railroads crossed the Ozarks, efforts to improve the region's waterways had all but ceased.

Until the era of FDR, the Ozark waters meandered to the sea pretty much in their natural state. The little water mills were but picturesque ruins by the 1930s. Except for a low dam on the White River between Forsyth and Branson, creating Lake Taneycomo, and a big dam at Bagnell on the Osage, making Lake of the Ozarks, the Ozark rivers ran as they always had.

The New Deal targeted the old slumbering Ozarks for federal improvement on a monumental scale. Prime-the-pump economics planned to flood virtually every river

valley with a Corps of Engineers reservoir. World War II delayed the Corps' plans. Many of the most beautiful rivers would be dammed in the decades that followed. Environmental and landowner opposition, and dwindling budgets for socialistic schemes have slowed, at least for now, the dam-building impetus. Flood control and hydro power benefits were exaggerated. Losses were under-rated or unmentioned. Some of the lakes have developed a tourist industry; others lie virtually ignored. The cost/benefit ratio of these grandiose projects would not stand scrutiny today.

Several of the most beautiful native rivers have been protected as National Wild and Scenic Rivers. Unfortunately, this was sometimes accomplished by condemning the property of small farmers. Other wonderful free-flowing rivers run through private lands managed in a manner compatible with preserving their natural beauty. Pollution from cities and livestock, unsightly gravel operations, and some kinds of timbering threaten some streams. Most of these indignities are correctable. A dam and its reservoir are an irreversible disaster.

◄ Turtle's eye view from the bottom of a spring-fed Ozark creek.

▸ Map turtle in the exceedingly clear waters of the North Fork of the White River.

The Ozarks is old and has dark secrets. The Ordovician and Mississippian limestones and dolomites that layer the region were formed at the bottom of oceans. The region has been high and dry longer than most places on earth so there has been time for a vast system of underground waterways and passages to develop. Rain seeps into the carbonate rocks along fractures and dissolves small and great spaces. When the rivers cut down below these water-filled cavities, springs emerge. The springs of the Ozarks are among the largest in the world. When the water table drops farther, the springs are drained and air-filled caves result. This karst landscape of sinkholes, losing stream beds, caves and springs, gives the Ozark rivers their distinct clear water and stable seasonal flow.

▲ Cave Spring on the Current River pours out more than 10 million gallons of water a day from a conduit 150 feet deep.

◀ Blue Springs near Powder Mill Ferry on the Current River. Divers have followed the spring back 250 feet deep to the limits of their equipment and nerve.

Greer Springs is not the largest spring in the region. In the primal, original, romantic sense, however, it may be the single most beautiful place in the Ozarks. It's actually two springs. A considerable stream issues from a cave, but a boil downstream in the bed of the branch contributes most of its average daily flow of 214 million gallons. Much of the Ozarks is quietly poetic. The environs of Greer Springs are Delphic, even disconcerting. Visitors, as they descend the steep path, hear a faint roar that grows more distinct as the light level falls. At the bottom of a green gorge, the chattering stops. Witnessed in the half light, the gurgling volcano of cold, clear water is a reminder that everything in nature is not the subject matter of calendars or greeting cards. Greer Springs madly babbles of subterranean rivers and lightless lakes, of the solid earth dissolved from within.

The botanical setting is lush. Other great springs are so near to rivers they are scoured by flood waters. This

spring emerges a mile from the Eleven Point River (where the spring's waters double its low water flow) and some 100 feet higher. The fifty-eight degree temperature of Ozark springs makes them fog factories. This deep canyon holds a fine mist long into a summer day. In winter, the valley is often in a cloud for weeks. Ferns, liverworts, and mosses coat the boulders rich green year-round. Watercress and some rare, out-of-range aquatic plants undulate in the swift, mineral-rich waters.

In spite of the misty and mystical atmosphere, several industrial enterprises have existed here. Captain Samuel W. Greer (he served in the Confederate Army) owned 1,001 acres in Oregon County around the spring that bears his name. His first water mill was right at the spring that today appears pristine, virginal. It operated until 1883, when a roller mill was built at the top of the hill. The big, weather-beaten structure still stands. A complicated arrangement of cables transferred power from a water turbine to the mill's machinery.

While working on the small dam at the spring that would channel the rushing water into the turbine, Captain Greer's twenty-three-year-old son, Lewis, was hit by a falling timber. He fell on the rocks in the boiling current and died. Lewis was just married, and his father had asked him to delay their trip to Oregon in order to work on the mill. Lewis's widow, Lydia, never visited the beautiful spring again. She is said to have often sat by an open window in the Greer home at the top of the hill, listening to the faint roar of the spring below.

Taking a last look at Greer Spring with its cave river, grey walls, gay with foliage, and all the harmony of color and form combined in the narrow canon . . . I recalled views on the Hudson River and in the mountains of Maryland, Virginia and Pennsylvania, and others out in the Rocky Mountains in Colorado . . . but amid all their wonderful grandeur and famous beauty, could remember no spot superior to this masterpiece of the Ozarks.

Cave Regions of the Ozarks and Black Hills,
Luella Agnes Owen, 1898

The spring-fed Ozark creeks are a joy to explore.

The incomparable wild and free flowing Ozark rivers.

Even in the bleak months the river country can be beautiful

4: Relics and Refuges

Frontier writers hailed the rapid settlement of the wilderness, but elegaically noted the decline of wildlife. The tone of Alphonso Wetmore in his 1837 *Gazetteer of the State of Missouri* is typical. After enumerating the game, "the ranks of which are thinned as settlements advance," he observed that "the visit of a solitary buffalo to his old haunts, or stamping-grounds, only reminds us of the wealth and luxuries of the red man when sovereign of these sparsely-inhabited regions."

Big game—elk, buffalo, bear, wolf, and panther—were eliminated from the Ozarks as elsewhere. Virgin forest melted before the ax. Unlike many other areas, it regenerated, but the second growth lacked magnificence. Urban sportsmen, often converts to the conservation movement, believed the hillfolk were responsible for the Ozarks' fall from a wild Eden. The locals, it is true, had a *laissez faire* attitude about game laws (and other laws), as did most frontier Americans. Even the chert in the river beds was blamed on hill country agriculturists. They did, after all, plow straight up a hill, if it suited them. Yet the larger changes to the Ozarks were brought about by the demands of exploding urban populations for meat, hides, minerals, and lumber.

Remembrances in county histories, and the rare writings of natives like Turnbo, reveal deep feelings of nostalgia for the loss of the wilderness and wildlife. Ozarkers today are, by and large, correct conservationists. Still, they are characterized in the press, from time to time, as unrepentant and unenlightened poachers and arsonists.

The myriad plants and animals that lived in the Ozarks survived the changes in land use remarkably well. Never glaciated, and above sea level longer than most places on earth, the ecology of the region is uncommonly complex. The rugged landscape contains microhabitats and relics from earlier climactic eras. Situated between western prairies, eastern forests, and southern

Civil War veteran Silas Claiborne Turnbo diligently collected tales of the early settlement of the Ozarks. He was able to self-publish only one small book of the stories. To his great disappointment, his large manuscript remained unpublished in his lifetime.

Though the old time hunter with his slow track dog and primitive ways has passed beyond this life, the report of the old time muzzle loader is seldom heard, the shambling bear is gone, the deer have nearly disappeared, the hundreds and thousands of wild turkeys are reduced to a mere handfull, yet the God-given gift of cool invigorating water still remains.

Silas Claiborne Turnbo, 1900

swamps, the region has a long species list. Isolation from development has sheltered this rich biota much as it has protected a quasi-frontier lifestyle. The wild Ozarks is a relic of both American nature and frontier culture. To those who care about either, it's a refuge.

The interaction between man and nature in the Ozarks is barely understood. Interpretations of this long story are often little more than fables spun by anti-humanists. In 1920, Carl Sauer lamented that regional geography was a field in decline. The best writings were then a hundred years old, the products of educated travelers observing the frontier. Sadly, today's efforts to comprehend the effect of environment on culture are mostly politically colored ideological maxims. To blame one segment of humanity for the adverse effects of culture on environment is not only unfair, it's untrue. The Ozarks is worthy of deeper and more impartial understanding.

Along the rivers big chunks of dolomite have tumbled into the clear water. From underwater crevices in the boulders, fish, turtles, and hellbenders eye you if you put on a mask and stick your head under the surface. Pick up a fist-sized piece of chert lying in a riffle. Out of its folds and pockets drip fifty nymphs, snails, helgramites, leaches, and maybe a half-grown madtom catfish. Small creatures want to hide. The Ozarks has many hiding places.

The Ozarks can be hard country to make a living from, but some things succeed. It's brimming, especially around the streams, with cold bloods (fish, frogs, insects) and little animals (opossums, raccoons, weasels, voles). There are birds, bats, and unusual plants left over from past, hotter and colder, climactic eras. It's not like Yellowstone or a rain forest. In the dissected, cut-over lands much of the old nature remains, but it's not a wilderness. Neither common or endangered species seem to care about such status, and neither do I.

The word "glade" evokes Old English. Visiting one throughout the year is a poetic experience. In spring, the glades are strewn with wildflowers. Collared lizards dash for cracks in the rocks in summer. Blazing star and purple coneflower color the slopes in fall. Winter reveals the structure of the hills the best.

The largest and purest complex of glades is in the Hercules Glades Wilderness. As elsewhere, the suppression of fire has allowed scrubby trees, especially the eastern red cedar, to invade the prairie openings. The U.S. Forest Service does perodically burn them to maintain their unique character.

Underlying the White River glades is a limestone-free chert. Ledges and slabs of this "cotton rock" are home to an intriguing group of animals normally found in the southwestern United States. Tarantulas, scorpions, giant centipedes, and roadrunners thrive in these Ozarkian miniature deserts.

On the next page are some portraits of glade reptiles. (Top left and then clockwise) Great Plains ground snake, collared lizard, six-lined racerunner, and a red milk snake devouring a five-lined skink. The milk snake and racerunner are also found throughout the Ozarks.

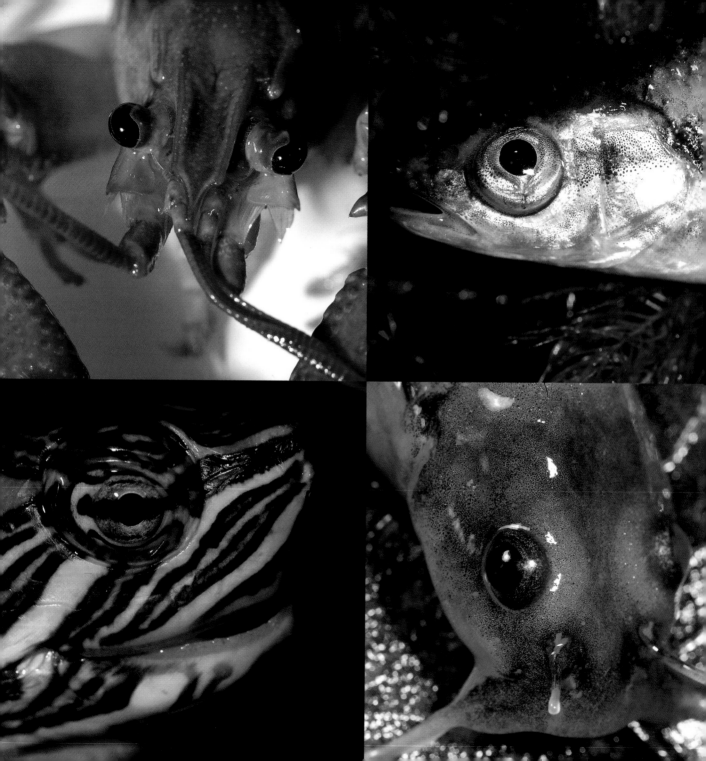

An Ozark river is home to an amazing variety of life

5. Local Color

The effort to connect the rocks, trees, rivers, and weather of a place with the character of its people was, not so long ago, in vogue. Local color writing sought that connection between soul and soil. Although a discredited academic literary form, local color writing is alive and well in Ozark regional magazines, local histories and feature stories in newspapers.

Silver Dollar City and Shepherd of the Hills Homestead and play, both in Branson, Missouri, and the Ozark Folk Life Center in Mountain Home, Arkansas, derive inspiration from the local color school of literature. City festivals about regionality remain popular. As corporate and media culture permeates every aspect of our lives and landscape, these often quirky celebrations of place have become especially vigorous and popular of late.

Even when regional themes were in literary fashion nationwide, not all writers and not all regions fit the style. The subordination of character to the limitations of one's circumstances goes against the upward mobility encouraged by the aspirations of our national version of the Enlightenment. Many Americans chafe against the chains of traditionalism and revolt against the limitations of place. Central to all visions and myths of the Ozarks is the compromise with success American-style that life in the rocky hills imposes.

The log cabin era settlers were, by temperament, suspicious of mankind's perfectibility and critical of the benefits, or at least the permanence, of a civilization founded on commerce. Immigrants to the hilly Ozarks have not much diluted this essentially 17th century Calvinist outlook. What kind of individual wants to struggle with thin soil and isolation? Randolph characterized them as "the most deliberately unprogressive people in the United States." Dreamers and schemers, hunters and herders fit in, and hard workers, too—those with few illusions or expectations. The deep Ozarks has not proven to be an ideal habitat for the immigrant fired up by ambitions of upward mobility. Believers in earthly solutions to mankind's dilemmas drift in, but soon find the place and the mindset discouraging, and leave.

Generations of the same family often lived in the same community, so that family history is intermingled with the landscape in an uncommon way. Life is integrated with the landscape in a natural way that is understood by everyone. Thus, the Ozarker is a kind of homespun Lockian who thinks of the landscape as an object that penetrates the mind and alters the man.

The Ozarks: Land and Life
Milton D. Rafferty, 1980

The rugged individualism of the early settlers has deep historical roots. Americans were invited to cross the Mississippi and settle what is now Missouri in 1788 by Spain, "as their prejudices against the English were a sure guarantee of their attachment to the Spanish interest." Not exactly, but the part about disliking the English was true.

The predominantly Scotch-Irish stock that made up the frontier class then had a long history of enmity with the Crown. A century or more before, the English had invited the Scots to settle in northern Ireland. After a century of occupation, the English hiked taxes and imposed tariffs on their woolen industry, causing a huge migration to America. "Scotch-Irish" means they were Scots, transplanted to Ulster, who then emigrated to America. (The Scots who stayed in northern Ireland have yet to make a lasting peace with the native Irish, as the nightly news reports.) Few who emigrated in the 18th century were Catholic Irish. Virtually all Scotch-Irish immigrants were Protestant, originally Presbyterian.

A century of savage warfare with the native Irish

prepared them well for the vicissitudes of Indian Wars and the Revolution in the New World—as if the Scots had ever known peace. Two thousand years earlier, the Celts, the tribe from which the Scots, Irish, and Welsh were all derived, were unconquered by the ancient empires. They were finally driven out of Europe and into the British Isles by the Romans. Celtic Scotland and Anglo-Saxon England have had stormy relations for a thousand years.

Carl O. Sauer characterized the indifference, even disrespect, that the Ozarkian Scotch-Irish had for strong central authority: "The American resident of the west bank of the Mississippi lived, as he had lived previously, by self-constituted order which he established and enforced in his pioneer community. His law was not determined by federal statute nor royal promulgation, but was the code of frontier society."

Under such circumstances, reinforced by the isolation imposed by the nearly road-proof terrain,

◄ Sketches from life in the foothills of the Ozark Mountains, Washington County, Missouri, by O. E. Berninghaus, 1920.

▶ Even outbuildings, like this corncrib on an abandoned Niangua River homestead, were of hewn log construction.

Within my own memory there were unregimented families in the Ozarks who lived by hunting and fishing, raising a few mast-fed hogs, growing a little corn, and distilling whiskey. There were hillfolk who denned in log cabins with dirt floors and no windows; men who slept on cord beds and killed deer with muzzle-loading rifles; women who used spinning wheels and wove cloth on homemade looms; minstrels who sang English ballads brought over by the seventeenth-century colonists; old settlers who believed in witchcraft and all sorts of medieval superstitions; storytellers who could neither read nor write, but who spoke the most interesting English in America.

Down in the Holler, Vance Randolph, 1953

this independent character was preserved. To a large degree the native Ozarker retains a distrust of big government. A more self reliant, but personable, people as a whole is hard to find anywhere.

The earliest settlers of Scotch-Irish descent came to the Ozarks from Kentucky and Tennessee primarily. They built their log cabins. Hunting was good. Their cattle and hogs could fend for themselves on the open range. A little corn to feed horses and make whiskey could easily be grown in the alluvial soil. Life was easy until the tragic disruptions of the Civil War.

The penetration of railroads, and later ridge roads, that connected the region with small trade centers, spurred a second wave of immigration from the Midwest, and even the eastern United States. New technologies and improved transportation allowed the prairies to be cultivated. Many of the earlier bottomland homesteaders built houses along the hilltop roads where the second wave of immigrants was buying land.

A pattern of small general farms emerged which

persists to this day. Row crops have declined and pasture prevails. Off-farm jobs are often taken, but a decidedly rural lifestyle still characterizes the region. The families of the pioneer stock intermarried with the post-Civil War immigrants. A Little-House-on-the-Prairie kind of culture was handily incorporated with the Daniel Boone background of the pioneer families. Farm folks, while scarcely subservient in outlook anywhere, have an especially independent mindset in the Ozarks. A trace of the untrammeled, free-wheeling outlook of the frontiersman here has blended with the diligence and responsibility characteristic of Midwestern agriculturists.

Generally omitted from the pop culture version of the Ozarker is the region's religious embrace of Christianity. A strong ethic derived from this faith guides their lives. Life in a region of scant resources is hard, but faith in the Lord is sinewy.

While most of the depictions of native Ozarkers are literary, Thomas Hart Benton painted the place and its people with a sense of their regionality. A native son of Neosho, Missouri, he did his best to leave his Ozark heritage behind. He dabbled in socialism and modern art in Paris in the 1920s. Coming to his Ozarkian senses, he realized that the left bank of the Buffalo River was better subject matter than the left bank of the Seine. Though he was to depict our rough, hard, Depression-era democracy throughout America, his hill country characters are prototypical. Hard-edged egg tempera paintings pose hillbillies, who hack oak or fiddle strings with equal mania, against an undulating hillscape with both scenic and erosional potential.

Vance Randolph captured the bodacious color of Ozarkers' speech at the same time Benton painted. Randolph's shelf of books lives with the language of a lively people caught in the cusp of massive technological change. His hillfolk are reluctant to trade in their vivid,

rich stories and traditional lifestyle for the manufactured and synthetic. They speak with more than a hint of Elizabethan English. They live and love and occasionally murder with the intensity of characters from Shakespeare. Such rambunctious behavior in real life, or written about, by rurals with small change and big talk was disdained by the Chamber of Commerce types who harassed both Randolph and Benton. Commercial, progressive America has a natural enmity toward impoverished country folks—especially well-armed rubes from the Ozark hills who are famous for making their own whiskey and for making fun of "furriners."

The stereotypical hillbilly is a line drawing and a literary simplification of the colorful regional characters loved by Benton and Randolph and, before them, Mark Twain and the southwestern writers. He resides in the

The traditional Ozarker has both a realistic grasp of human nature and a wry sense of humor. Hillfolks' legendary conversational banter and sharp observational skills have endured the influx of modern media jargon and the institutionalization of English to a surprising degree.

netherworld of media, not in the hills and hollows of the true Ozarks. Hillfolk, a PG version of the hillbilly, can be found in several of the sentimental but sympathetic novels of Harold Bell Wright. A living version of the local color hillfolk can be found today skillfully making authentic crafts or apple butter at Silver Dollar City. Often hillbilly and hillfolk traits are mixed together. They are stereotypes with a ring of truth, entrenched bits of Americana not likely to disappear from our popular culture.

The Ozark hillman of Benton or Randolph was not identical in every respect to his representation in art. That can be said about all art. But, in this case, the artists and their subject were in large philosophical accordance. These folks in the flesh and the painter's and penman's representations were united in a deep and abiding suspicion that what modernity takes away may not always be worth the price. Indoor plumbing, the automobile, and radio were welcomed into the Ozarks. The loss of the old songs and sayings, the lessening of family bonds, and giving up personal freedoms of the frontier were lamented in both life and art.

Gaudy ambitions are out of place in the hard scrabble hills. Rain and tears have scrubbed the place clean of fugitive hues. It's a limited palette, but the feelings and colors are intense and saturated. The local color of the Ozarks is earth-toned and subdued. The rivers run transparent over pale-orange chert beds and gray-green in the pools. Fated by geography, and a bit faded from the hard light of historical experience, real Ozarkers know their place and themselves as few people do.

Hillman with muzzle-loading rifle, Vance Randolph photograph. (Lyons Memorial Library, College of the Ozarks)

'Coon hunter with favorite hound

Still photo from Harold Bell Wright's 1919 movie version of *The Shepherd of the Hills.*

Violet Hensley, Silver Dollar City's fiddle maker.

Nixa, Missouri's, annual Sucker Festival.

Here are a few images of some of my favorite Ozark traditions. May the sounds of the fiddle, the baying of the hounds, and the celebration of shoaling redhorse never vanish from the hills.

Besides the British Isles, the only other significant place of national origin of immigrants to the Ozarks was Germany. A few people of French descent remain in the St. Francois Mountains, reminders of the French colonization of the 18th century. Tiny colonies of Italians, Swedes, Poles, and Bohemians arrived in the 19th century. The northern tier of the Ozarks, along the Missouri River and radiating up the Osage, Gasconade, and Meramec rivers, was heavily settled by Germans beginning in the 1830s. They prospered in the loess-covered hills and fertile river valleys. Significant aspects of their heritage have been preserved.

In the vanguard of Teutonic immigration were people of noble birth, lured by Gottfried Duden's romantic published accounts of the region. Later German immigrants were farmers and skilled artisans. They built stone and brick houses, tended vineyards from which good wine was made, and crafted handsome walnut furniture. Until several decades ago, many older people preferred conversing in German.

The landscape of the German Ozarks is pastoral and

pleasing. Pin-neat villages, above which rise the spires of old but well-maintained Catholic or Lutheran churches, are always a pleasure to visit.

6. Far from the Madding Crowd

Not so long ago, most people lived "far from the madding crowd." Urbanization is recent. Industrialization moved us, slowly at first, from farms and villages to cities. The abandonment of country life accelerated in the 20th century. Suburban children rarely have a grandpa's farm to visit anymore. Soon the family farm crisis will vanish as an item on the nightly news as the pastures are subdivided or sold to corporate holdings. The modern mega state disdains our authentic country roots. Media culture is about immediate sensations, not rural recollections.

Long before the farm crisis, rural themes were in decline as fashionable subject matter. London intellectuals in the mid-18th century such as Samuel Johnson derided pastoral poets like Thomas Gray. The great lexicographer exempted Gray's *Elegy Written in a Country Churchyard* (1751) from his criticisms: "to say he has no beauty would be unjust. The *Churchyard* abounds with images which find a mirror in every mind, and with sentiments to which every bosom returns an echo."

While art about country life has never completely died out, its acceptance by urban taste makers has been provisional. In 1874, Thomas Hardy borrowed a line from Gray's *Elegy* to title his Victorian novel. Nearly a century after Hardy's novel was published, *Far from the Madding Crowd* was made into a film starring Julie Christie and Alan Bates (1967).

Generally, rural life in modern literature and entertainment is either grotesquely harsh or unrealistically sentimental. Life in the boonies is ridiculed or satirized following Dr. Johnson's general critique of "graveyard poets". Not that these criticisms of lapsed taste and excessive sentimentality are always untrue. There is plenty of country kitsch. But a corresponding cultural examination of urban myths and sentiments is rarely made. Hick isn't really chic in high culture, and hasn't been for a long while.

Popular culture locates pulp romances in rural areas. Myriad middle class households are decorated in what is called "country" style. Such references are not "far from

▸ When the Corps of Engineers flooded Ozark river valleys with reservoirs, graves were dug up and moved to high ground. This relocated cemetery from the Table Rock project is in Taney County, Missouri.

Far from the madding crowd's ignoble strife,
Their sober wishes never learned to stray;
Along the cool sequestered vale of life
They kept the noiseless tenor of their way.

Elegy Written in a Country Churchyard
Thomas Gray, 1751

the madding crowd" at all, but pleasant, mass market, escapist fictions. The culture of the rural Ozarks, sliced and diced and dammed as it is, still retains an authentic flavor of traditional rural attitudes. The landscape, from semi-wild forests to marginal farms and ranches, is decidedly primitive. This fact sets up an endless conflict between the region's conservative landowners and urban preservationists. Both are branches of the same anti-modern tree, but they fail to see that they share philo-sophical roots. Internecine quarrels are often the most savagely fought. Each camp has suspicions of the other's motives and competence. Though alike in a desire to turn the clock back in the remote Ozarks, they disagree on precisely at what time to stop. Natives of the region long for the freedom from government characteristic of the frontier. Urban romantics wish to recreate in a re-created pre-settlement Eden. Both groups love the Ozarks, both are well entrenched in their own political realities and myths; neither is likely to completely get its way. The place is likely to remain as its image portrays it. Rafferty again summarizes it well: "(The Ozarks is) a significant and distinct region of both geographic and cultural

resistance to progress."

There are physical evidences of probably every culture that has ever inhabited the Ozarks, an amazing amount of which is seeable from the roads or findable a few steps off. The Ozarks changes, but more is left behind of the works of man than in most busier and geologically mutable places. Pits and piles of rock remain where the French dug for lead in the 1700s. Burial cairns of stones piled up by the aborigines are found on bluffs high above the rivers. The rocks of both the French diggings and the Indian graves are lichen-covered but recognizable, although pushed around by trees and, in the case of the cairns, farm lads deludedly looking for buried treasure of the Spanish conquistadors. If a shard of pottery or a rusty Dutch ax are unearthed by New York construction workers, it's news-at-eleven. Indian and pioneer relics are strewn across the Ozarks everywhere. Practically every farmer who followed a mule had an Indian rock collection. The "perfects" were in cigar boxes in the house; the broken ones in coffee cans in the barn.

Not just bone, stone, and concrete are left behind.

▲ The spirit of fundamentalist Protestantism remains strong in the Ozarks, but brush arbor revivals and creek baptisms, once common in rural areas, are seldom held today.

Almost every kind of building ever built can be seen, though often in a melancholy state of repair. True, none of the wood and hide shelters of the first inhabitants remain, but plenty of archaeological traces exist in the river bottoms. The preferred habitats of the earliest inhabitants, Ozark caves, are often floored by a ten- to twenty-foot deep mixture of earth, bones, mussel shells, burnt wood, and flint chips produced by the making of weapons and tools.

There are yellow and black and red billboards along the roads directing the tourist to "See Indian Burial Cave." In the shadow of the sign, slowly rotting in the weeds, is a flaking sheet of plywood. Once it announced the comforts and low rates of a tourist court that has been closed for thirty years. Now it is home to either a blue tailed skink, a copperhead, or both. Five miles farther on, the little rock rubble buildings still stand, sheltering a miscellany of old bottles, broken farm utensils, a 1928 water-stained Sears catalog, and ragged patchwork quilts. The dripping-letter, painted-over sign, once used at a filling station, says "Antique."

The whole Ozarks is antique. A disappointment, if by that word one means cherished, polished cherry wood furniture, gilded picture frames with old oil paintings, and delicate ceramic and glass objects miraculously handed down for 200 years without a chip. The Ozarks is antique in another way. The Ozarks is a museum of mistakes displaying a little of what all of us were, are, and probably always will be in our human totality—the failures, the marginal, as well as the successful and prosperous. As monumental cliffs sculpted from the residue of ancient seas lie around river bends, the architecture of the overlooked and forgotten of American culture is just around the bends of blacktop roads.

Early in our country's history, we were embarrassed at our lack of ruins compared to Europe. The Ozarks is a treasure of eroded landscapes and a culture whose roots are tenaciously established. To dismiss the experience of the frontier is to forget where we came from. "Old fashioned" should not be a blanket pejorative. Under some tarnished traditions are hard and durable concepts. Beneath the bright varnish of many progressive notions are pitted and rusty and base motives.

Ozarkers are not in possession of solutions to mankind's woes, nor do they claim to be. They are heirs to a long experience of a life of struggle and have a larger-than-average understanding of human frailty. The Bible, whose teachings most are familiar with, is supremely realistic about the limits of human knowledge and the tragic circumstances that are humanity's fate. To view this outlook as naïve and primitive is an error. The rural areas of the United States have many citizens of similar outlook and experience as well. Not enough

◄ The archaeological history of the Ozarks reveals that it was home to small bands of Indians who utilized a wide variety of its natural resources. Before European settlement, it was not densely inhabited, as the hillier regions remain to this day.

attention is paid to their durable wisdom. Why, they, and we, should ask, are the environments they live in considered beautiful and yet their culture thought so deplorably backward and unfashionable? Did the spirit of romanticism take a wrong turn somewhere, leading us from an adventurous quest to understand both the natural world and man, to a bizarre, pagan worship of nature and primitive "Others"?

Both an appreciation of natural beauty and rural Christian culture are likely to endure in the deep Ozarks. Perhaps, in time, there will be some realization that these two value systems are not as mutually exclusive as they seem today. The Ozarks is a superb refuge for the plants and animals that came before us. Those folks that make it their home are not as different or obdurate as some think. They are good Americans, if slightly old fashioned in their outlook. I think they often have something valuable to contribute that is in short supply. It takes real faith, humor, and character to have survived here. We don't have a surplus of those pioneer virtues.

The Ozarks has long been a great place to escape, far from the madding crowd. I expect it will remain so.

The Ozarks preserved a bleak-sweet landscape that once characterized much of America. The region is not, of course, changeless. For a long time it was a backwater, out of the main currents of progress. There was an elegaic side to this isolation, but it could work hardships on the residents. Rural poverty is rarely, in and of itself, poetic. Log cabins leak. Old iron bridges can give way under the weight of a school bus. Low water crossings are deadly when flooded. One room schools were often run on skimpy budgets. In spite of these difficult material circumstances, the Ozarks has long been home to some of the most interesting, independent, and colorful men and women America has produced.

Bridges across Arkansas's Buffalo River are few and far between. Many of the cars that come down the mountain and around the curves on state Highway 14 are topped by canoes. The river is a floater's dream, sporty riffles alternating with green pools, under soaring soft gray cliffs. Officially, a National Wild and Scenic River, gravelbar leisure on the Buffalo can be civilized and scenic as well.

There are only a few authentic water mills left in the United States. Dawt Mill is on the North Fork River, near the hamlet of Tecumseh. Old Dawt Mill is a great spot to expose film and expose your kids to a nicely proportioned mixture of history and nature.

◀ A couple of Tom Sawyer types (Strader and Ross Payton, a few years back) head for the hills along Arkansas's Buffalo River.

▼ View of the Buffalo National Scenic Riverway.

▲ Alice Wright and her great niece, Morgan, on the old Y bridge over the James River at Galena. Mrs. Wright's husband was a float guide on the James River before Table Rock Lake.

▶ Crystal Payton on our lost Niangua River farm.

Mark Twain had it right. He thought the best country was along rivers and the most interesting folks those who coped with the promise, peril, beauty, and destructiveness of moving waters. In Twain's youth, rivers were the veins of commerce and America was largely rural. The Army Corps of Engineers has since attempted to convert the nation's waterways to a gigantic piece of plumbing, and the politics of favoring urban growth has driven the populace off the family farm. Finding the modern world not to my taste, I was able to find some relatively unmolested streams in the Ozarks and folks who could be dropped into a Twain yarn without much adjustment.

For a decade after high school, I eked out an existence dealing in Indian relics and old books, playing no-limit, table-stakes poker over a pool hall, fishing and collecting snakes, and photographing the Ozarks. My boon companion was Lothair, an enormous Weimaraner. Fine animal that he was, he was a poor herpetologist. Dogs imitate their masters, so Lothair was fascinated by

snakes. He never learned, unfortunately, to distinguish the fanged varieties from the non-venomous bluffers like the hog nose playing 'possum in the photograph. He survived both copperhead and cottonmouth bites, but barely. I often ponder what improvement in my material circumstances would have resulted had I realized back then the boom market for photographs of Weimaraners dressed up in funny clothes. Lothair's muzzle was so scarred by the snakebites he wouldn't have been a pretty enough model anyway.

When environmentalism became a cause in the late 1960s, my photographs became fashionable. For a time I was employable as a creator of photo exhibits which were intended to foster "environmental awareness." That career suddenly vanished after I became a plaintiff in a lawsuit to stop Truman Dam on the Osage River.

While still gainfully employed, I met and married Crystal. Being a cosmopolitan and sophisticated type from Bonner Springs, Kansas, she had less enthusiasm than I about roughing it in the Ozarks on reptile-collecting and photographic

80
OZARK PHOTOGRAPHS
BY
LELAND PAYTON

THE OZARK RIVERS
OF MISSOURI

safaris. Having two boy children definitely altered my pelagic, rural wanderings. We traveled, but looking for underpriced antiques to sell.

We stumbled through the child-rearing years, dealing in antiques and writing on popular culture. Why TV lamps and kitschy, tacky artifacts, after years spent putting my existential spin on nature? Looking over my old photographs, I find an alarming number of images of yard ornaments, souvenir stands, and old filling stations. Truth is, I always loved such tasteless, "bad" stuff. It's a miracle I ever fit into the conservation/ecology program as briefly as I did.

My image of a red milk snake scarfing up a skink, on which my old environmental exhibit brochures rest, is a tad vivid and violent for eco-sumerism. I snapped the picture of an Arkansas souvenir stand, on which our pop-culture books lie, while headed to delta wetlands on assignment for *Audubon* magazine.

Is there a synthesis possible

between idealized nature and the often vital, but disdained culture of the common person? These two bodies of work I've done (all the pop culture stuff is co-written with Crystal) may seem schizophrenic. Look closely. There is a little more grain and grit in my nature photographs than in most. My images of carnival chalks and flea market kitsch come off with a poignant beauty sometimes. Could you guess Pieter Brueghel is a favorite painter and William Faulkner a favorite writer? The world is a lot of things and they seem to be what they are, all at the same time, sacred and profane alike. If not achieving the Greek ideal of eternal truth and classical beauty, Brueghel's and Faulkner's works have humanistic beauty and existential endurance.

The Ozarks is thought to be a place of sublime natural beauty and endangered wildlife by some. Other versions have it the home of a species of debased humanity. Are such polarized judgements as appropriate for artists as sharp-focused curiosity and a scale of values with a thousand shades of luminous gray?

Lens & Pen Press
3020 S. National, #340
Springfield, MO 65804

Write for a listing of Leland Payton photographs for sale.
Visit our website @ http://www.beautifulozarks.com